*Innocent, **Your Honor***

*"Your wife! Your best friend! Their attorney!"*

# Innocent, *Your Honor*

A Book of Lawyer Cartoons

by Danny Shanahan

Harry N. Abrams, Inc., Publishers

ACKNOWLEDGMENTS

*Thanks to Lee Lorenz, Bob Gottlieb, Tina Brown, David Remnick,*
*Bob Mankoff, Anne Hall, Stanley Ledbetter, Emily Votruba, Andy Friedman,*
*Marshall Hopkins, Christopher Sweet, Isa Loundon, Jane Cavolina,*
*everyone at* The Cartoon Bank, *and everyone at* The New Yorker
*(especially the dervishes in Checking and Legal).*

Editor: Christopher Sweet
Editorial Assistant: Isa Loundon
Designer: Robert McKee
Production Manager: Norman Watkins

Library of Congress Cataloging-in-Publication Data
Shanahan, Danny.
Innocent, your honor : a book of lawyer
cartoons / by Danny Shanahan.
    p. cm.
Includes bibliographical references and index.
ISBN 0–8109–5902–X (hardcover : alk. paper)
1. Lawyers—Caricatures and cartoons.
2. American wit and humor, Pictorial. I. Title.

NC1429.S49A4 2005
741.5'973—dc22
                          2004023453

Printed and bound in China

10 9 8 7 6 5 4 3 2 1

Harry N. Abrams, Inc.
100 Fifth Avenue
New York, N.Y. 10011
www.abramsbooks.com

Abrams is a subsidiary of

LA MARTINIÈRE
GROUPE

UNCLE BERNIE'S LITIGATOR FARM

*To Wade, Cate, Uncle Lou, David, Forrest,*
*Jen and Em, Rachel, John M., John D., Warren, Kevin, Rick*
*and Barry, Esquires all. If I forgot you, sue me.*

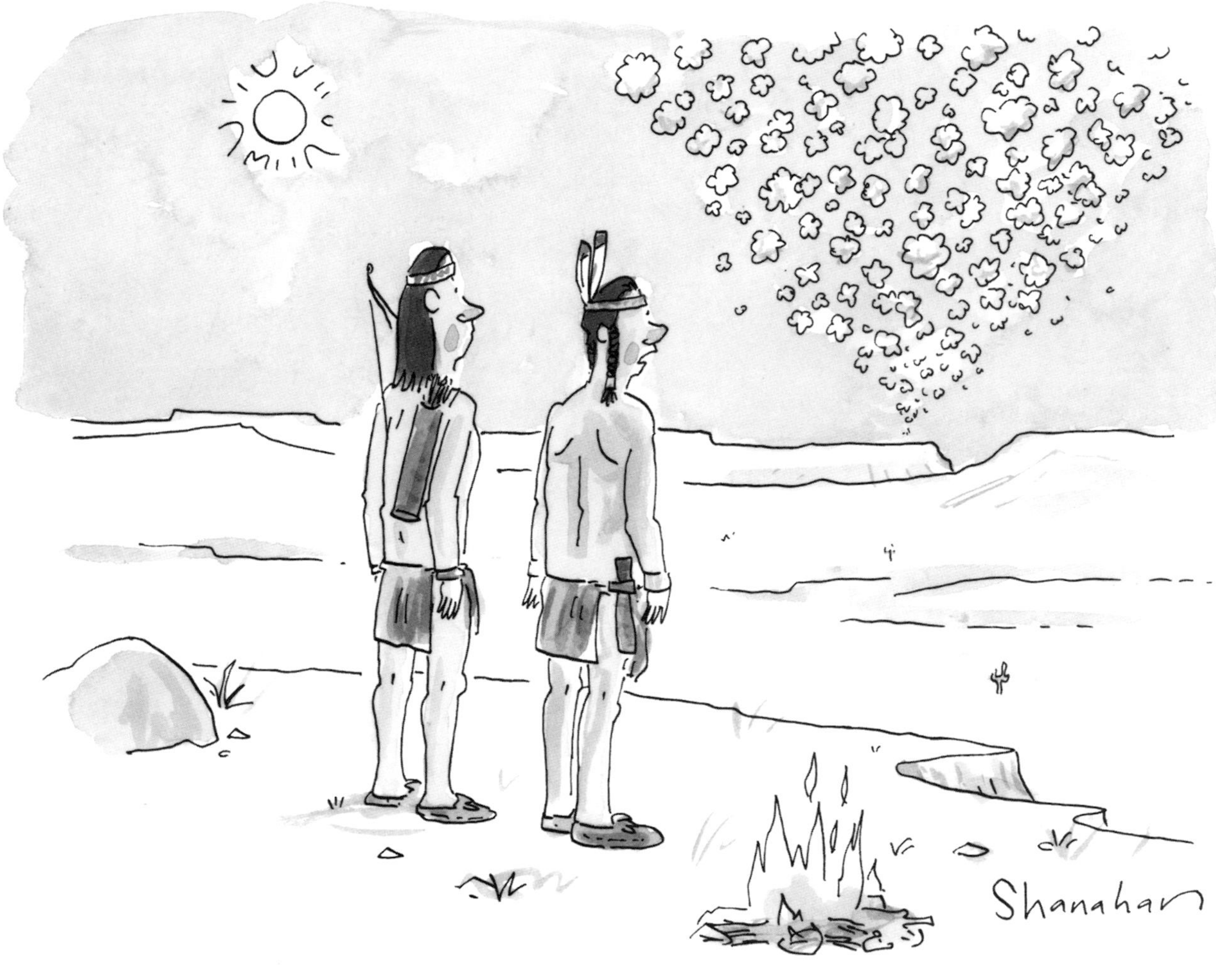
Shanahan

*"It's from my attorney."*

*"Wait! First, his attorney."*

# Introduction

"The first thing we do, let's overbill all the losers."
—*Shakespeare's lawyer*

Ladies and gentlemen of the jury, may I ask you a question?

What is it about lawyers? Why is it that we all hem and haw and rack our brains, struggling to remember that wonderfully funny cat/dog/golf/in-law joke we heard just last week, yet when we're asked if we've heard any good ones about lawyers lately, the floodgates open, spilling out zinger after zinger after zinger:

"An attorney walks into a . . ."

"How many lawyers does it take to . . ."

"That was no lawyer, that was my . . ."

"Janet Reno? Not with your . . ."

What is it about these sometimes articulate, ofttimes compassionate, and always well-dressed people that makes them such an easy target? And if attorneys are such a guaranteed fish-in-a-barrel laugh for all of you out there in lawyerland, does the same hold true for the professional cartoonist, someone like yours truly, someone whose livelihood, whose very existence depends on what I like to call "humor"?

## YOU BET IT DOES!

As far as I'm concerned, nearly every single thing about lawyers is flat-out, fall-down, bust-a-gut (file-a-lawsuit) FUNNY! What could possibly be more wacky, more madcap than the fees they charge, so outrageously inflated that they could single-handedly bring back transatlantic blimp travel? Or those briefcases, so humoungous they could comfortably house a little girl's tea party, little girls (and stuffed, glassy-eyed guests) included? Or their professional sartorial creativity, so well-honed as to elevate striped tie buying and three-piece suit dry cleaning to a widely admired, tax-deductible art form?

The list goes on and on. There's "legalese," the only language ever invented for the sole purpose of keeping its translators in business (and in BMWs, private clubs, and colonials in Connecticut). Celebrity trials? Fun-neee! Celebrity lawyers? Even funnier! Verbal gymnastics? I laugh myself senseless at just the thought of all those endless, circuitous arguments and rebuttals of Marxian intricacy and complexity (think Groucho, Harpo, and Chico, not Karl).

With the legal profession, there is simply no need to mine deep and hard for the cartoon mother lode. There are countless nuggets just lying there on the surface, settin' where any gol'durn fool can pick 'em up, dust 'em off, and waltz into town, ready to cash 'em in at the nearest mercantile. That's where I come in.

For the past seventeen years, I've been fortunate enough to have staked my small claim in the pages of the *New Yorker* magazine. Every day I hunker down in my studio for a little light prospecting. At the end of the week, I wash out my pans, saddle up my burro, and take my haul down to the Big City. I find myself a meter with some time left on it, hitch up my ride, spit in the dust, and drag myself through those storied swinging elevator doors. I mosey up to the receptionist's desk where Stanley the barkeep pours me a stiff one. "Thanks," I say. "Don't mention it," says Stan. He looks me over expectantly, and I know what's coming. "Anything lawyerly this week?," he asks. Every week the same question; every week the same answer: "Yep, Master Stanley, quite a few." We nod and smile, pleased as always by our little ritual. Then he grows serious, his smile faltering. "Will you say it?," he asks, his eyes pleading, insistent. "Sure, why not," I reply, and a broad grin creases his face. He leans forward in anticipation. "Pro bono," I say, and instantly he begins to giggle. What the hell, I think. I let him have it. *"Habeas corpus,"* I say, and his laughing intensifies.

*"Nolo contendere!"*

*"In flagrante delicto!"*

"LEGAL ANALYSIS!!!"

Stanley's on the floor now, braying with law-induced laughter, shaking uncontrollably. Tears are pouring from his eyes. I decide to stop the bombardment; he's had enough for the day. In a few minutes, I'll head down the hall to meet with the cartoon editor. He'll weigh my cartoons, bite down on a few, pronounce them legal tender, and buy them for the magazine. But for this one moment, the quivering chucklehead in front of me is all that matters.

I shift my saddlebags and grin.

Fool's gold.

—Danny Shanahan

*"A unique and stirring plea, counselor."*

LEGALADE
50¢

Shanahan

"*Two boys from legal to see you.*"

Shanahan

"*What the firm needs, Harrison, are more hardworking, dedicated eunuchs like yourself.*"

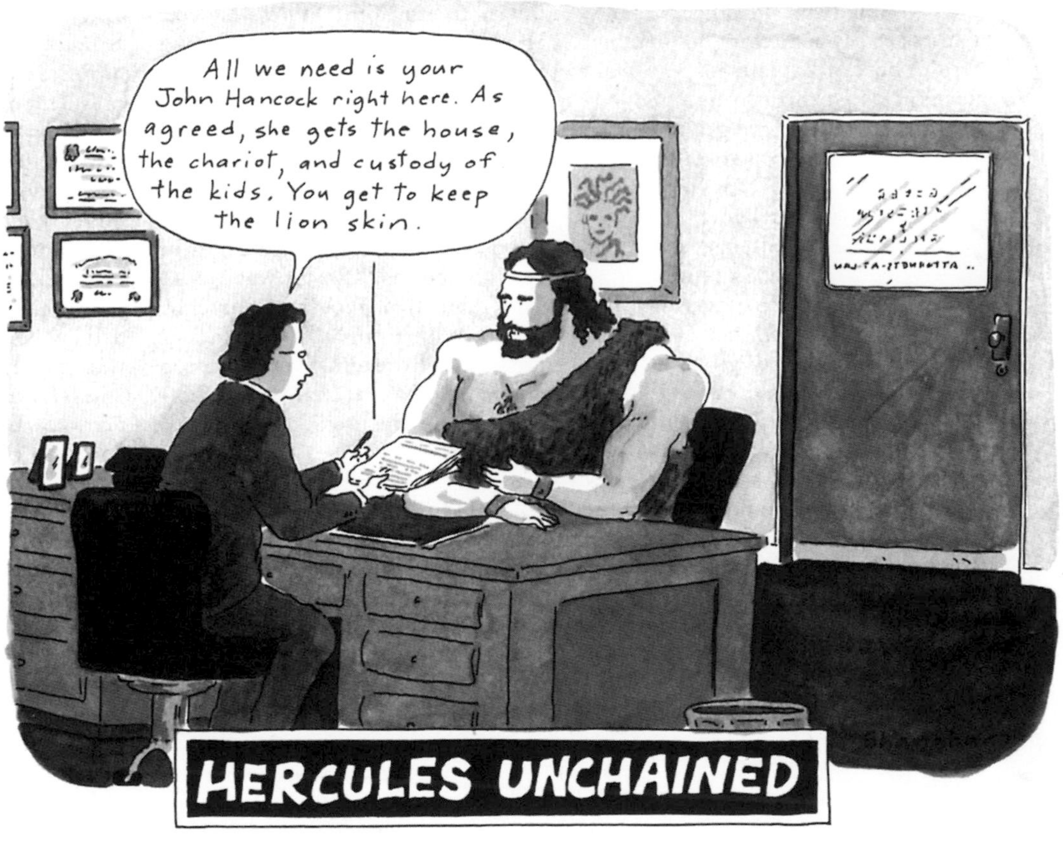
All we need is your John Hancock right here. As agreed, she gets the house, the chariot, and custody of the kids. You get to keep the lion skin.
HERCULES UNCHAINED

"Three yummies, a pat on the head, and a 'Good doggy.' That's my client's final offer."

*"Hi! I'm Edward Sadlon III, your trial-size lawyer."*

"I wouldn't—there's an awful lot of scary-sounding legalese."

*"We're slapping you with a stress suit, pal!"*

"*The ones just out of law school are especially frolicsome.*"

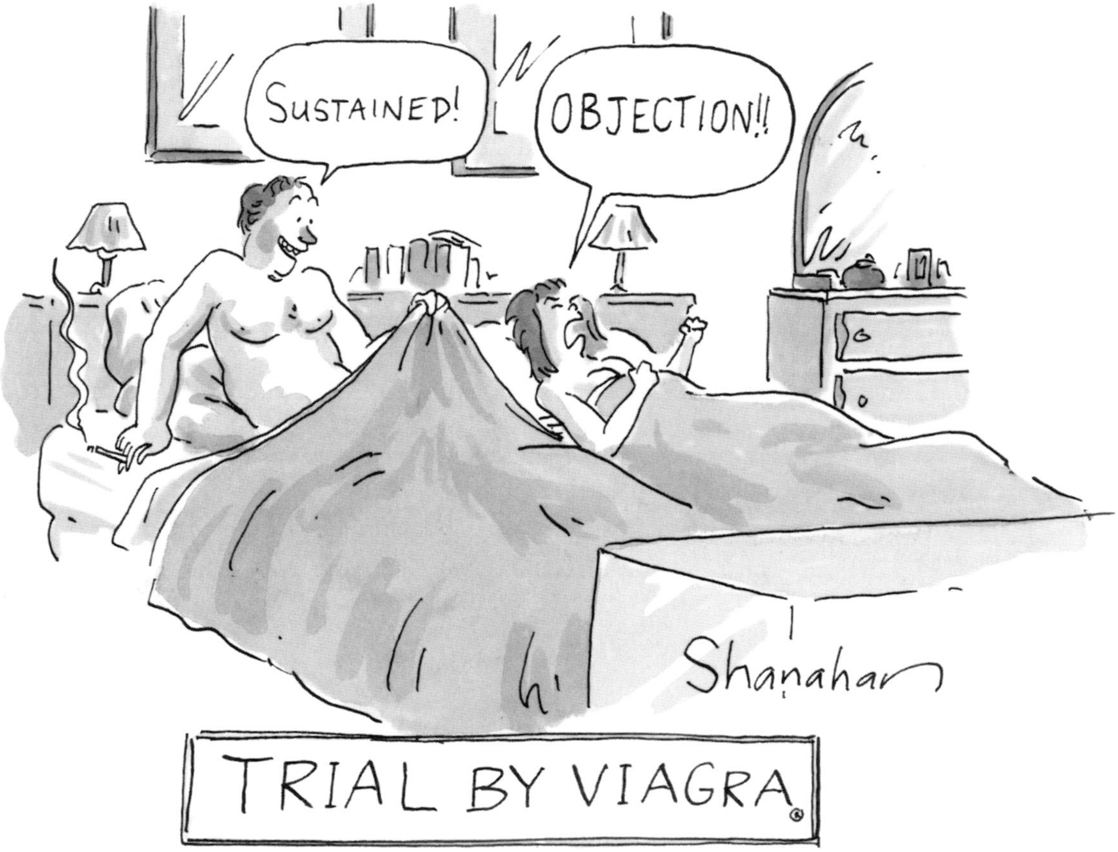
SUSTAINED!
OBJECTION!!
Shanahan

TRIAL BY VIAGRA

*"Damn thing's supposed to be attorney proof."*

"*With grades like these, you'll never afford a decent attorney.*"

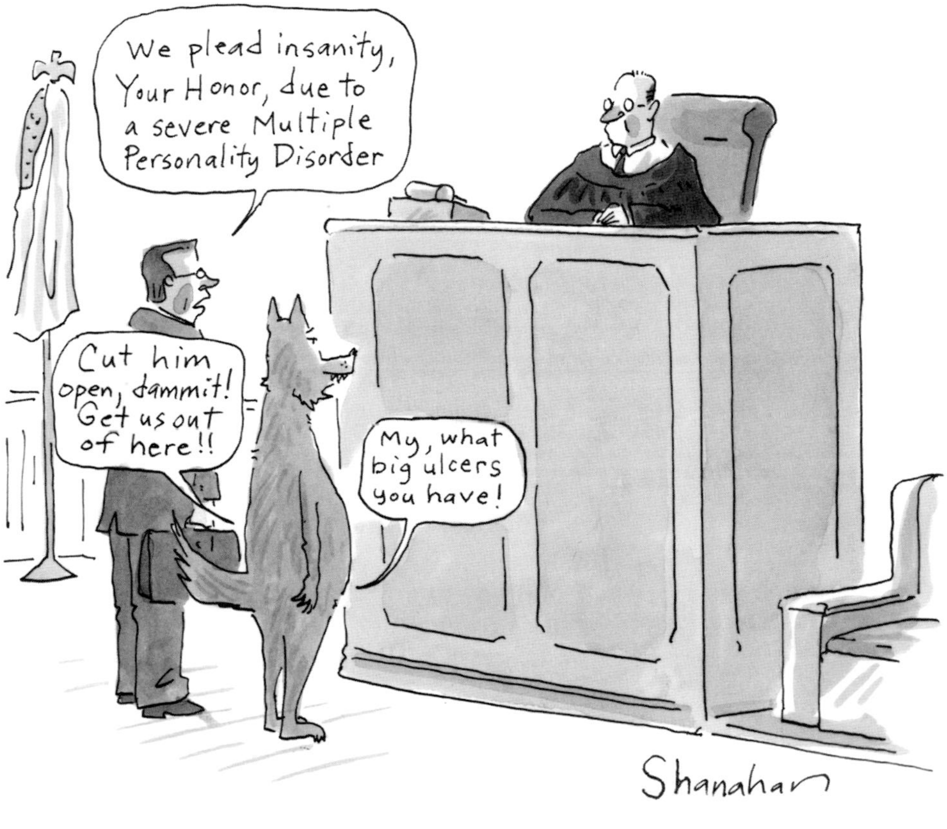
We plead insanity, Your Honor, due to a severe Multiple Personality Disorder
Cut him open, dammit! Get us out of here!!
My, what big ulcers you have!
Shanahan

*"Do you need an attorney, little boy?"*

Shanahan

"*And because a princess can't be forced to testify against her prince, they lived happily ever after.*"

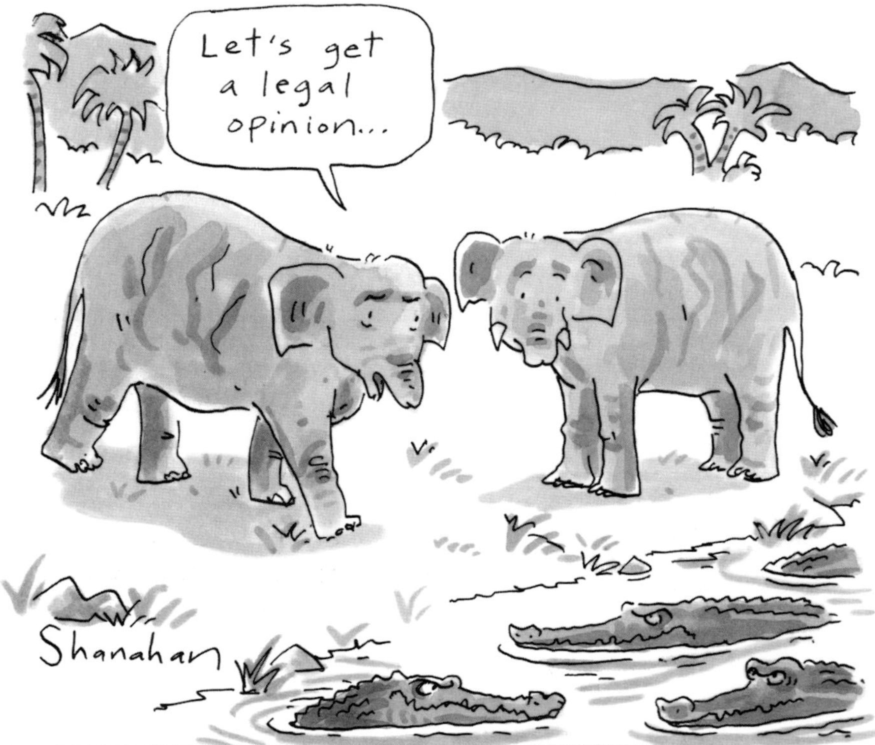
Let's get a legal opinion...
Shanahan

HOW THE ELEPHANT GOT HIS TRUNK

"I'll have my people subpoena your people."

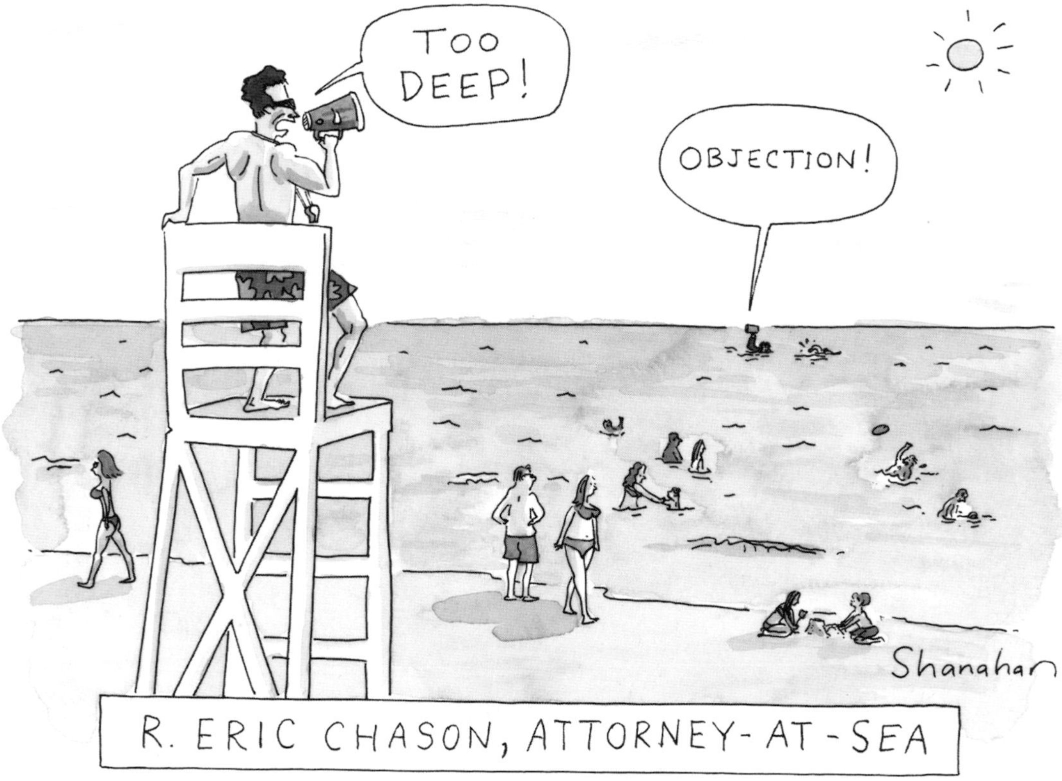
TOO DEEP!
OBJECTION!
Shanahan

R. ERIC CHASON, ATTORNEY-AT-SEA

*"Gotta run, Peter. A new client is on his way up."*

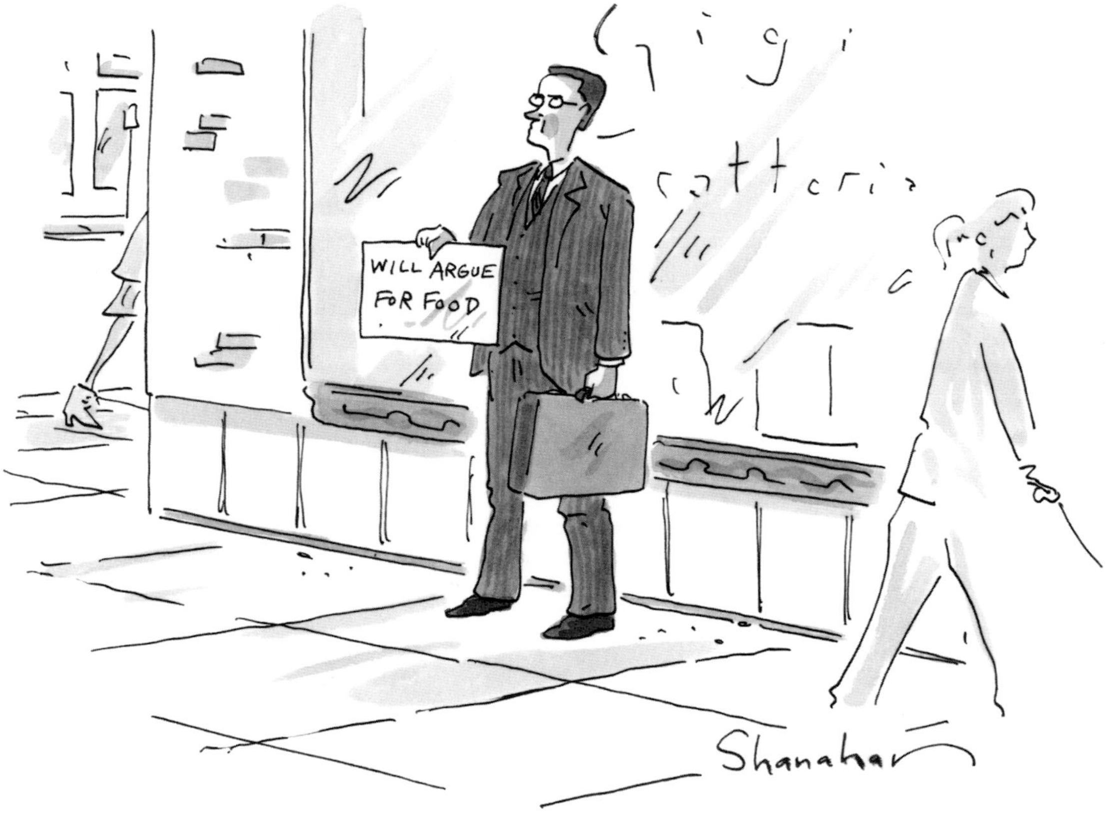
WILL ARGUE
FOR FOOD
Shanahan

*"Take your best shot, counselor."*

"*In the future, son, everyone will be an attorney for fifteen minutes.*"

"Since this is only your first offense, and you've been found not guilty, I'll be lenient in my sentencing."

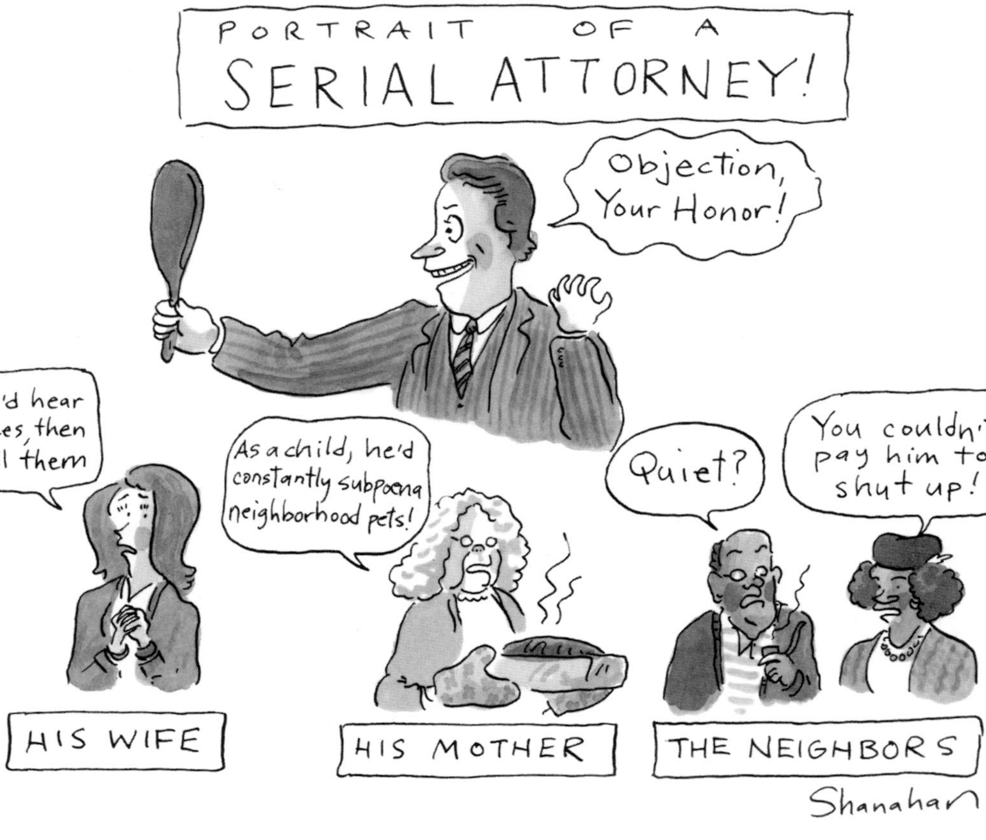
PORTRAIT OF A
SERIAL ATTORNEY!
Objection, Your Honor!
He'd hear voices, then bill them
As a child, he'd constantly subpoena neighborhood pets!
Quiet?
You couldn't pay him to shut up!
HIS WIFE
HIS MOTHER
THE NEIGHBORS
Shanahan

*"Sustained!— Prosecution will kindly refrain from flaring its hood."*

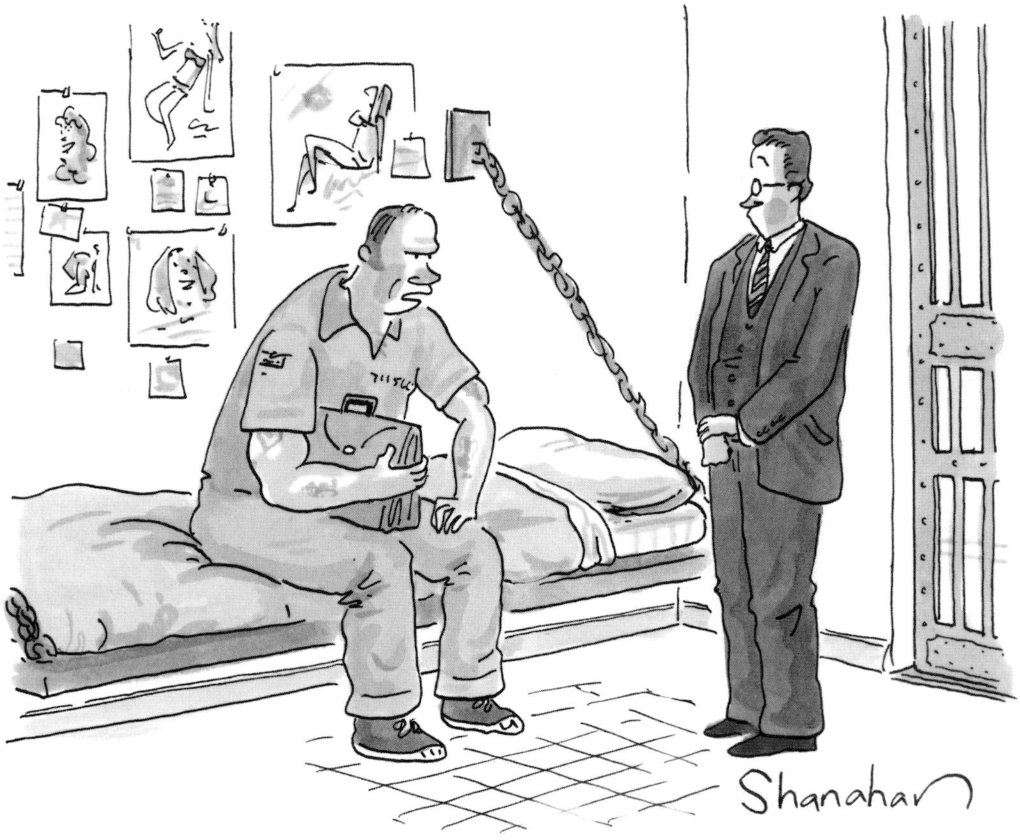
Shanahan

*"I'm taking your case."*

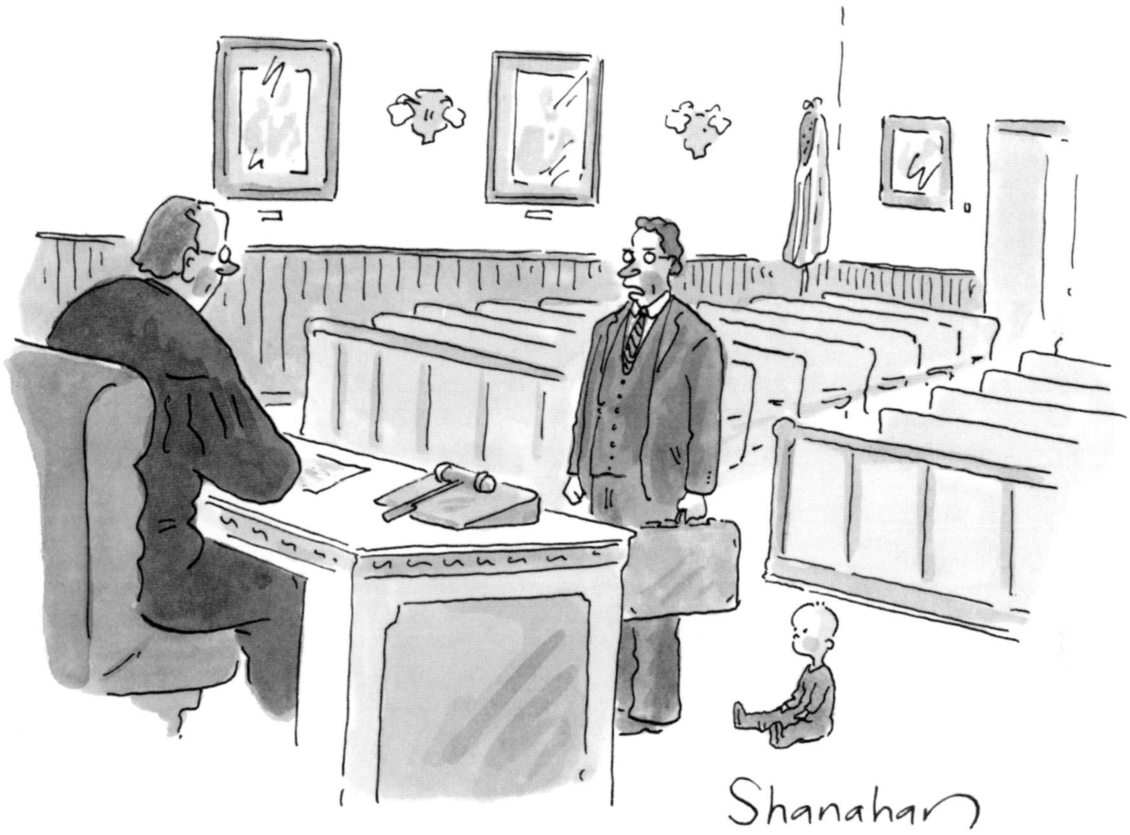
Shanahan

*"Innocent, Your Honor."*

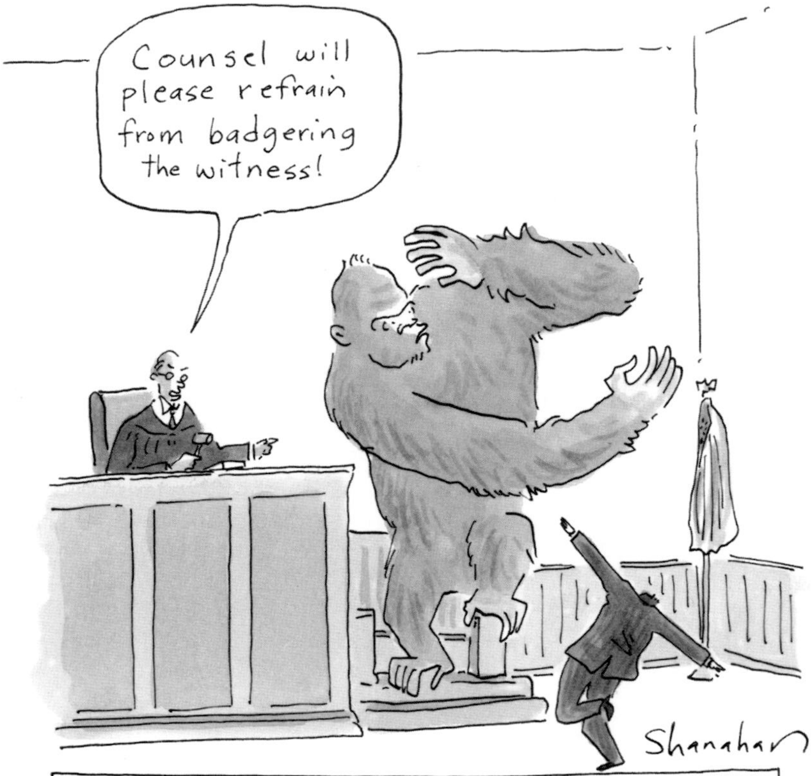
Counsel will please refrain from badgering the witness!
Shanahan

KING KONG vs THE CITY OF NEW YORK

"Do you have a good attorney or a bad attorney?"

Shanahan

MISTRESS DOMINATRA, ESQ.

"Although my client was well aware of the falling crime rate, Your Honor, he chose not to be trendy."

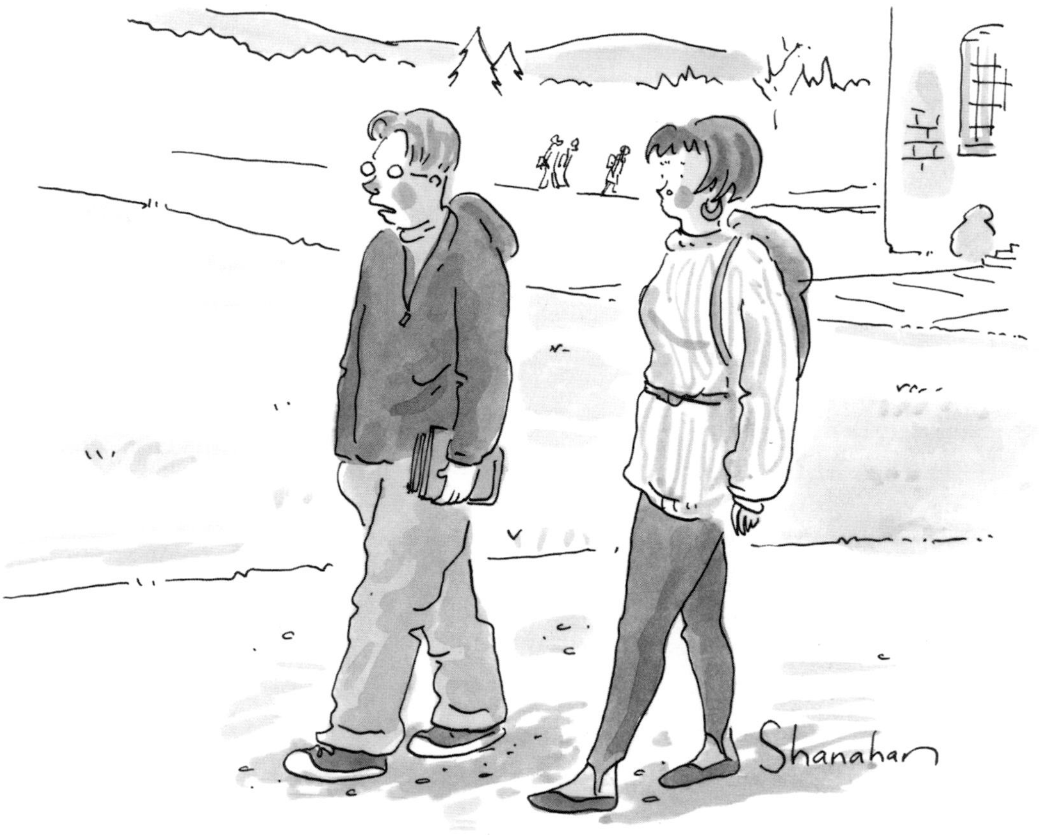
Shanahan

*"I'm pre-legal analysis."*

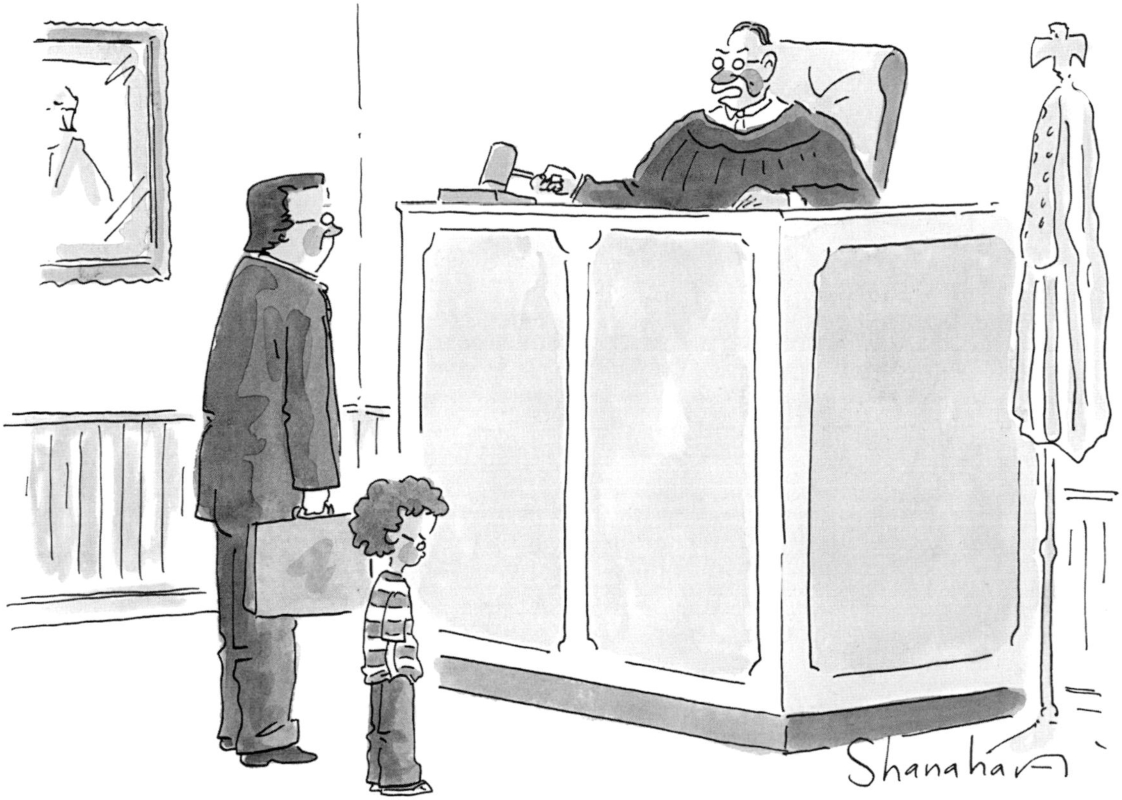
Shanahan

*"Five years hard candy."*

"*I know what Ally McBeal would do.*"

"*I shot a man in Reno, just to watch him die. After that, law school was pretty much a given.*"

*"Does it hurt when my attorney does this?"*

*"And just to be on the safe side, tongue of attorney."*

"He's across the street at the bus stop, but if you send in a high-powered attorney, we can take him from here."

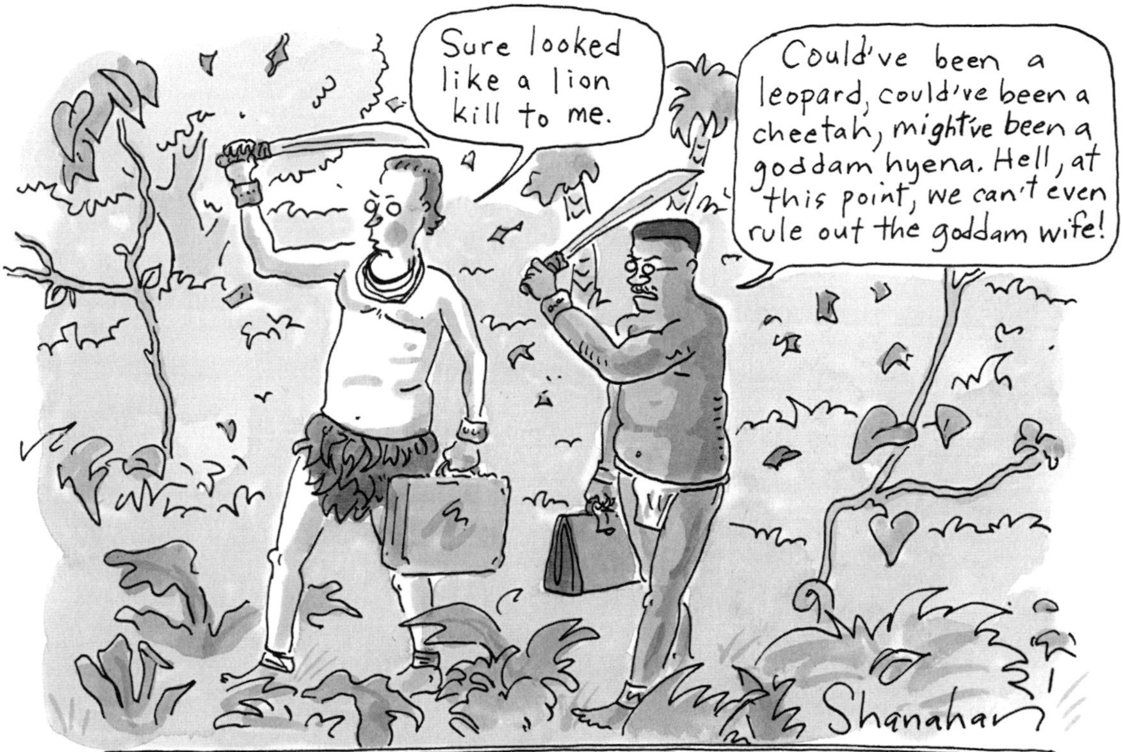
Sure looked like a lion kill to me.
Could've been a leopard, could've been a cheetah, might've been a goddam hyena. Hell, at this point, we can't even rule out the goddam wife!
Shanahan

THE LAWYERS OF THE JUNGLE

*"A word to the wise, counselor: Anymore of these tiresome displays of ethics, and I'll have you jailed for contempt."*

"*Congratulations, counselor—it's a baby boy, with a full set of teeth.*"

""I'd like to level with you, Mrs. Ravenscroft, but there's no legal precedent."

"*Objection, Your Honor! The prosecution is combining dog years and people years in a callous and deliberate attempt to confuse the witness.*"

"*What are you—some kind of justice freak?*"

*"My, Grandma, what a big-shot attorney you have."*

"*He may be only a junior partner, but remember—his mother destroyed half of Tokyo.*"

"*Fortunately, Mr. O'Brien, a sucker's attorney is born every half a minute.*"

"*I may be a jackal-headed god of the underworld, Janet, but I'm also your lawyer.*"

"*Give me one more chance, Rachel. I'll go straight, and quit my lawyerin' ways.*"

WADE "GATOR" RUBEN, TAX ATTORNEY

"*They swabbed and tested every kissed ass in the firm, and Orlitzky's DNA was a perfect match.*"

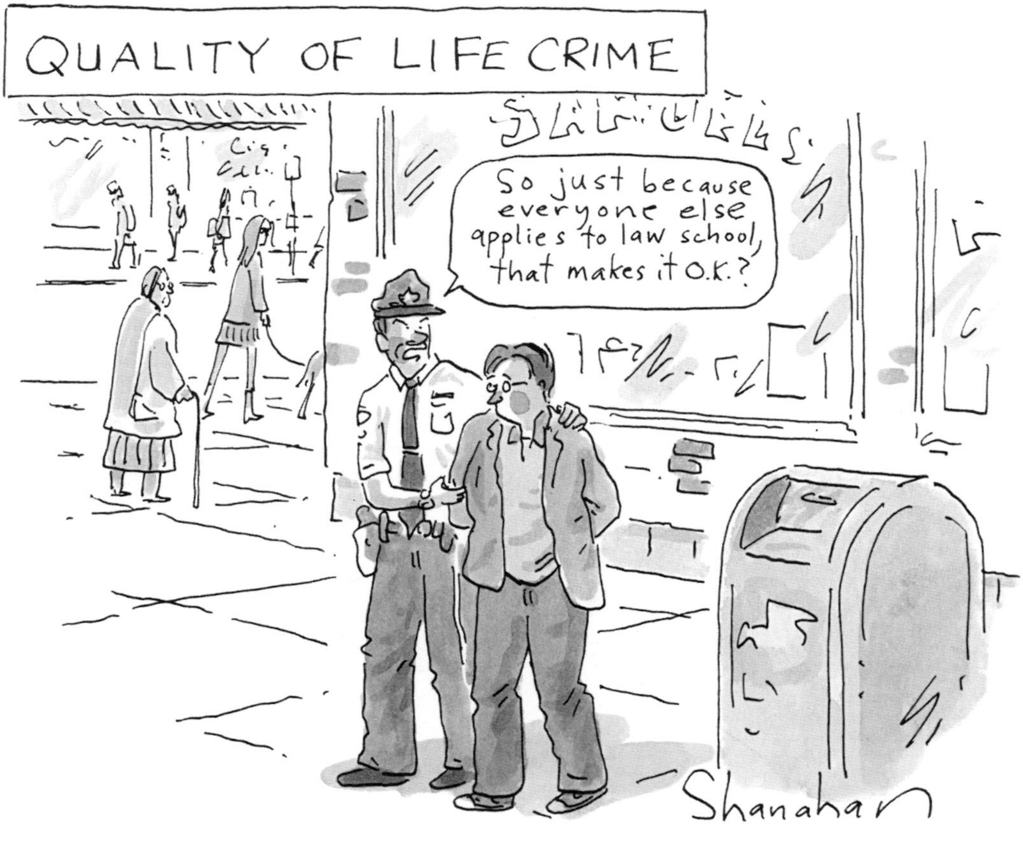
QUALITY OF LIFE CRIME
So just because everyone else applies to law school, that makes it O.K.?
Shanahan

"Get with the back beat, counselor!"

*"Will your client marry my client?"*

Shanahan

"Sorry we're late, but Kenneth Starr subpoenaed our regular babysitter."

Shanahan

"I'm sorry, gentlemen, but I feel it would be best for my client and I to continue to exchange furtive, sidelong glances."

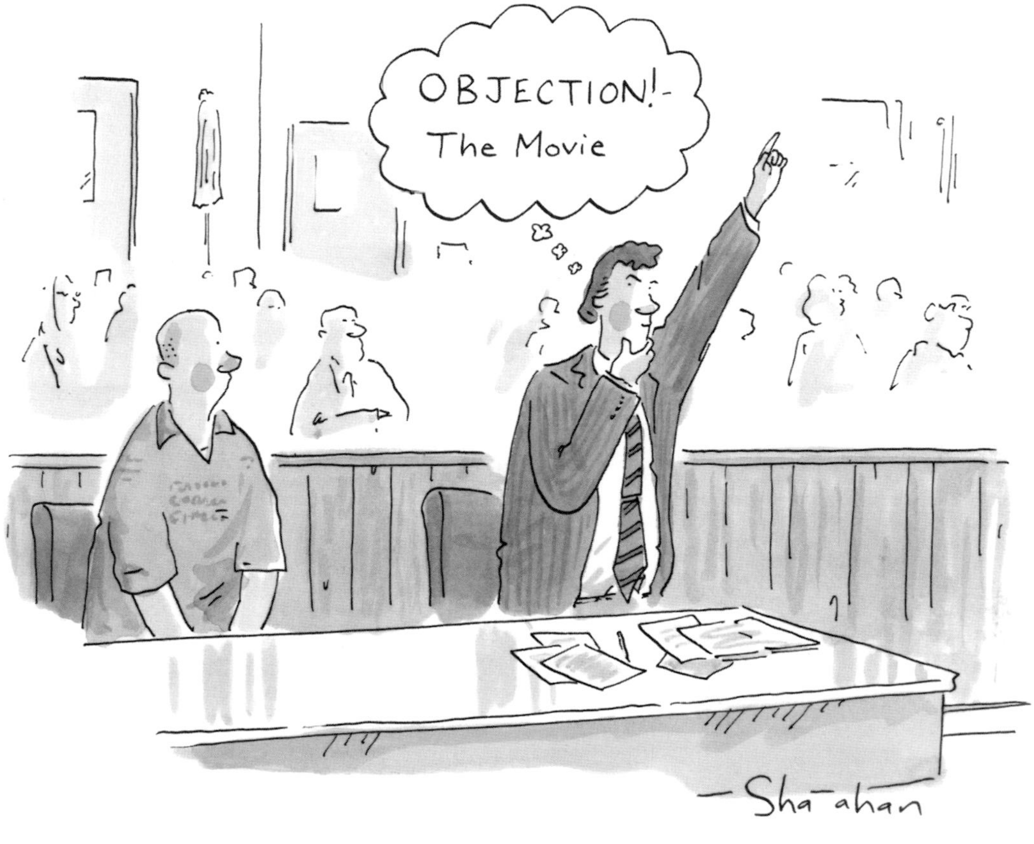
OBJECTION!-
The Movie
Shanahan

*"We prefer to remember him the way he was, before he passed the bar."*

MARVIN, MARVIN,
MARVIN, MARVIN
&
MARVIN

ATTORNEYS · IN · DEEP

Shanahan

*"I'm sorry—I never discuss my clients with their mothers."*

"*Run, Alison! Anything but a head shot only angers an attorney.*"

*"And before you mail your valentines, please make sure your attorney reviews the sexual harassment waiver."*

"*Objection, Your Honor!—the prosecution is dodgeballing.*"

"*But I gave my lunch money to the special prosecutor* yesterday."

*"Gun* PLAY, *Your Honor, gun* PLAY!*"*

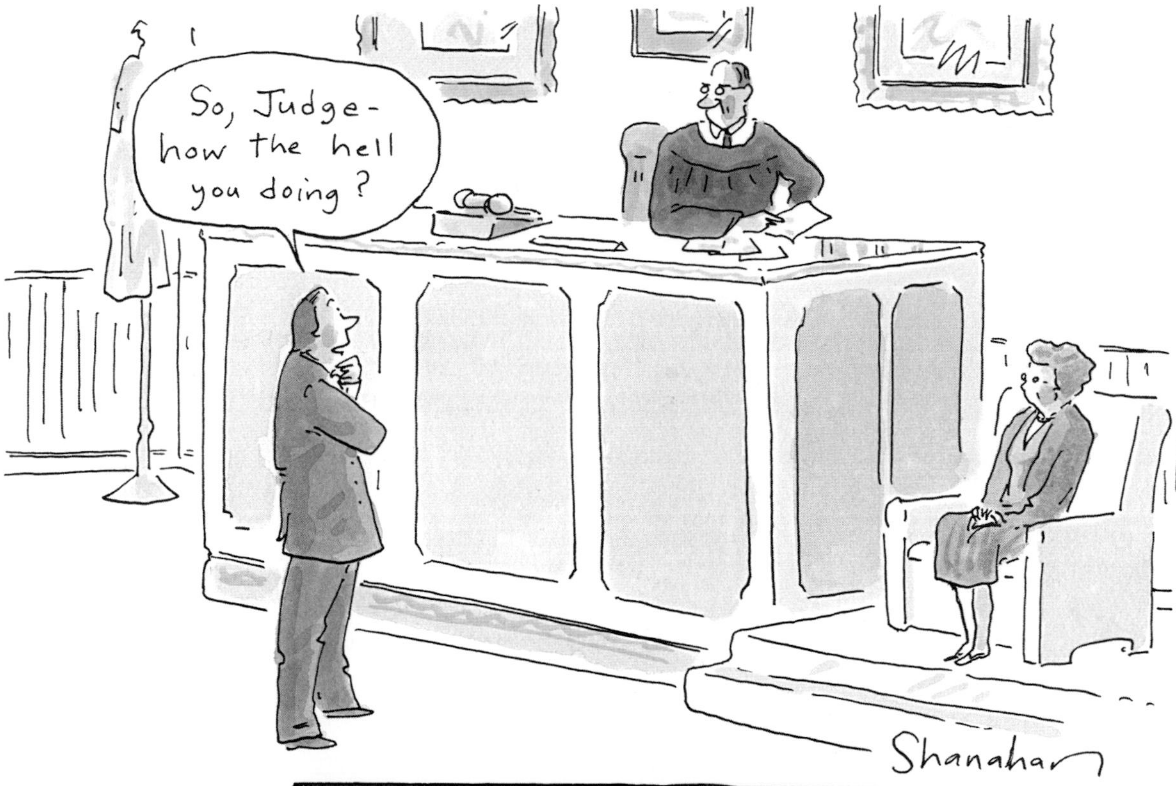
So, Judge-
how the hell
you doing?
Shanahan

**LAWYER'S BLOCK**

"*Damn!—And we were this close to an attorney-friendly settlement.*"

*"Excellent—let's run it through legal."*

"*I lost it in a legal minefield.*"

*"And I got this scuff in a nasty jostle with an overzealous public defender."*

"It wasn't a carcinoma at all—it was just an itty-bitty attorney."

"*And, in exchange for his testimony, your client gets to pick something nice out of our catalogue.*"

"Hi, Mom—did you get my subpoena?"

"There's been talk of having you disbarred."

"*I'm going out for beef chow mein—want anything?*"

"*Nothing from the governor, but I did manage to get you a tax extension.*"

"*Now with a firm twist, I'll remove his attorney.*"

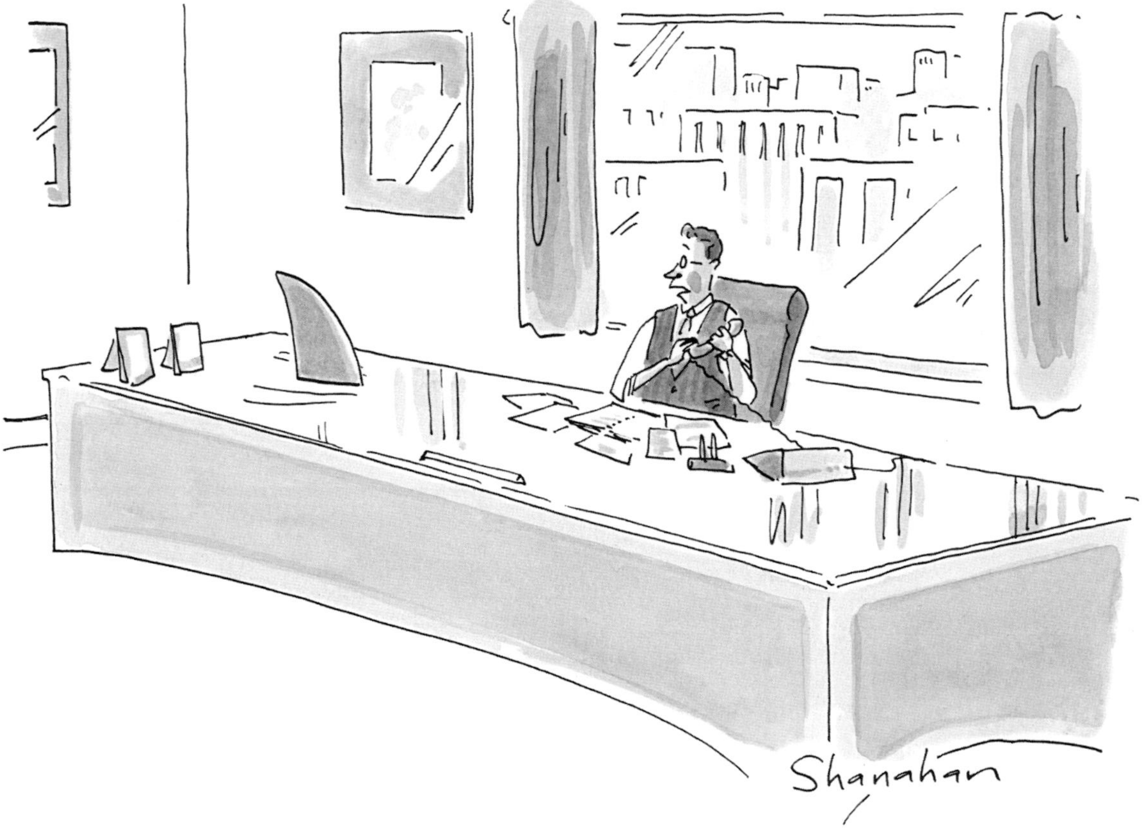
Shanahan

*"Counselor? Is that you?"*

"Do you need more time to prepare, counselor?"

"*I think we should accept the prosecution's generous offer of a coin flip.*"

"Sorry Mr. Gross, Mr. DeVries, but the firm has decided to go with the earthy, down-home fingerpicking of Ms. Aimee Parker-Grossman."

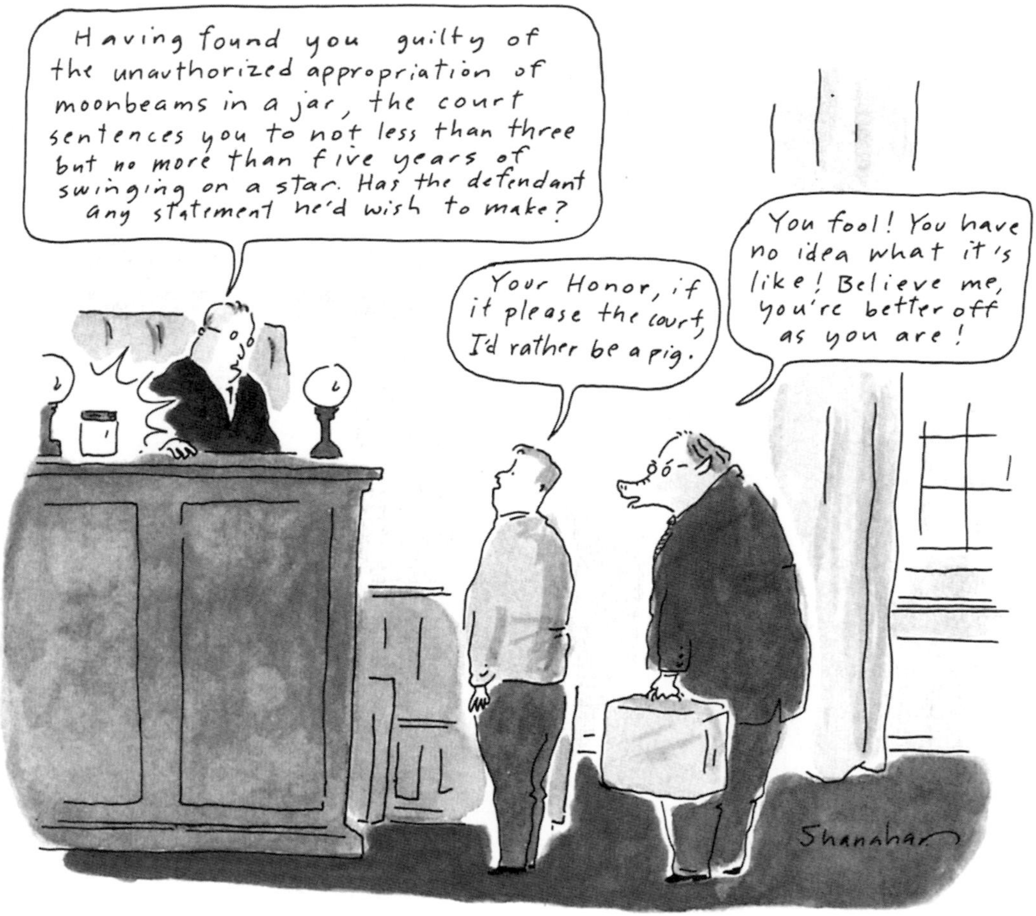
Having found you guilty of the unauthorized appropriation of moonbeams in a jar, the court sentences you to not less than three but no more than five years of swinging on a star. Has the defendant any statement he'd wish to make?
Your Honor, if it please the court, I'd rather be a pig.
You fool! You have no idea what it's like! Believe me, you're better off as you are!
Shanahan

"*Great news! I've found someone to feed your cats.*"

*"It doesn't scream 'Girlie Lawyer'?"*

"We're due in court in ten minutes, Counselor—use the big hand!"

*"I touched a bible once. Yowch!"*

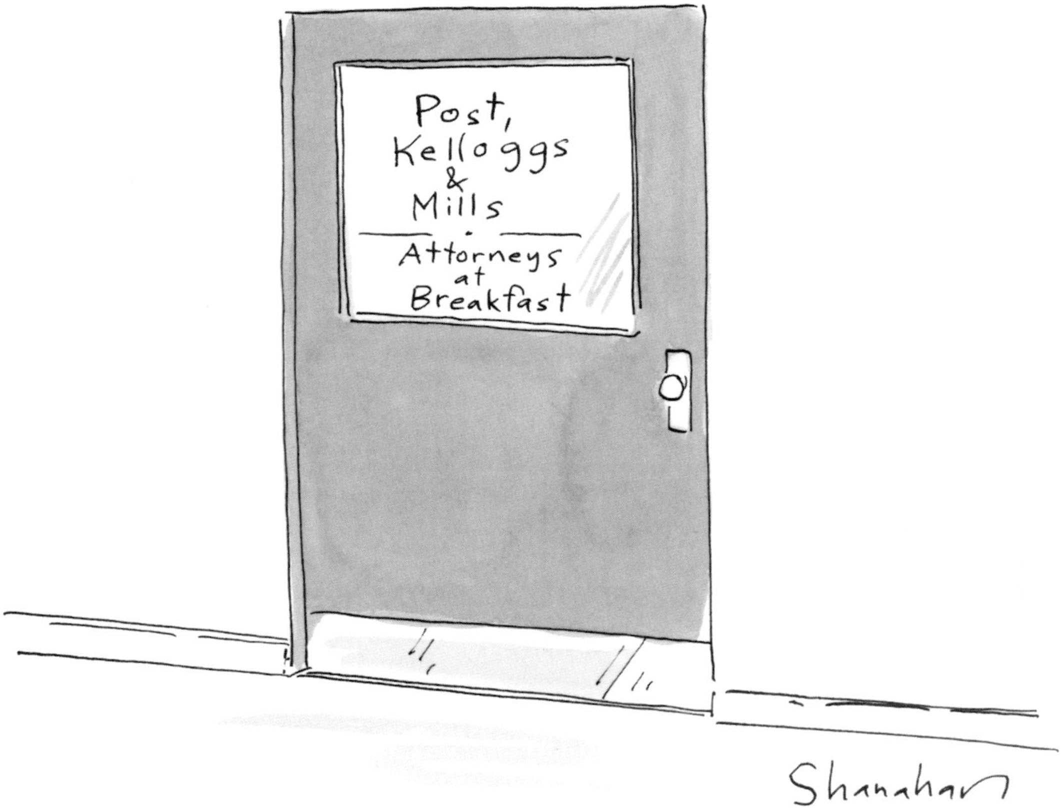
Post,
Kelloggs
&
Mills
Attorneys
at
Breakfast
Shanahan

"I've sent last minute treatments to all the major studios."

"Hell—let's exhaust our illegal options, too."

*"And I'd like to get out of this damned suit!"*

*"It's a nasty little law, Mr. Taylor. Fortunately for you, I'm a nasty little lawyer."*

*"And thanks to you, I have to buy myself a brand new lucky tie!"*

*"Careful!—she'll become enraged if she senses the slightest threat to her clients."*

"You heard the lady, buddy—she already has legal representation!"

"*The governor's granted your stay, but the zucchini fries tonight.*"

Shanahan

"My client is completely rehabilitated, Your Honor, in a grabass sort of way."

Shanahan

"It sure would be swell if your last words didn't mention that eyewitness who recanted her testimony, the con that confessed to your crime, the DNA test that proved your innocence, or the fact that I slept through most of your trial."

*"Bad news—your DNA was delicious."*

*"May I remind the witness that a simple 'I see you' will suffice."*

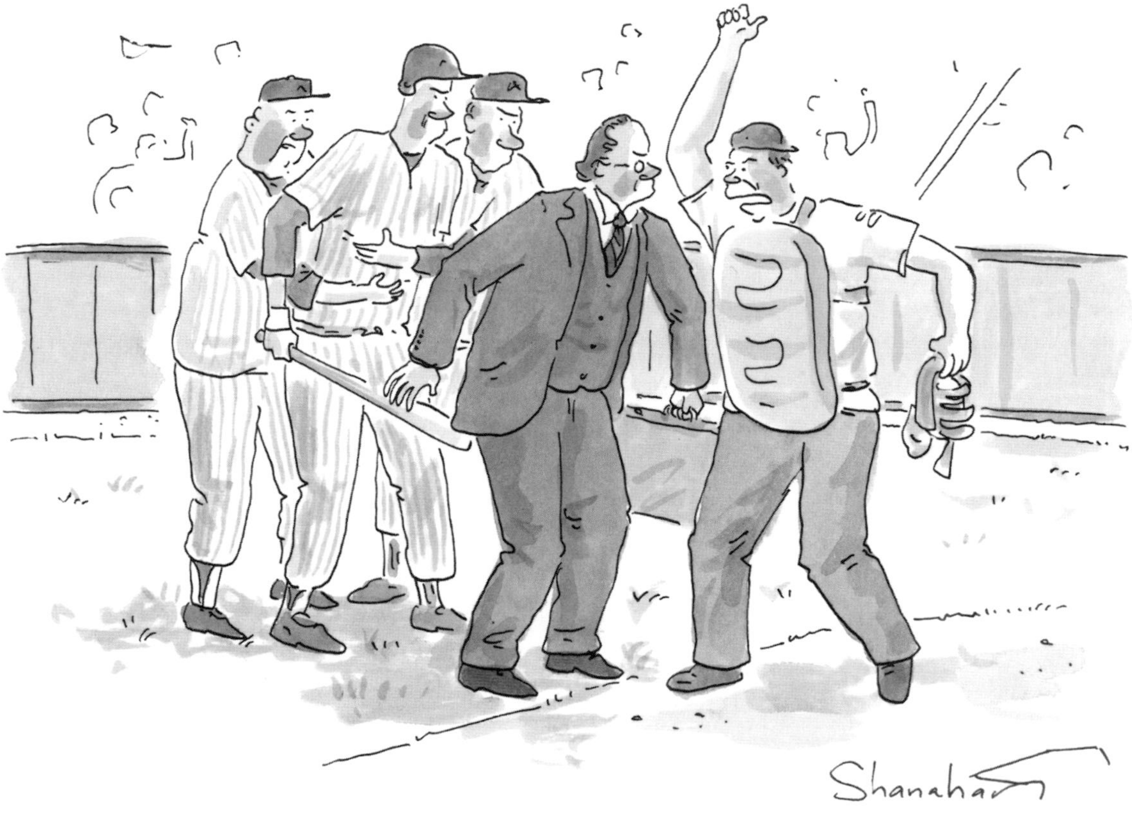
Shanahan

*"Counsel is outta here!"*

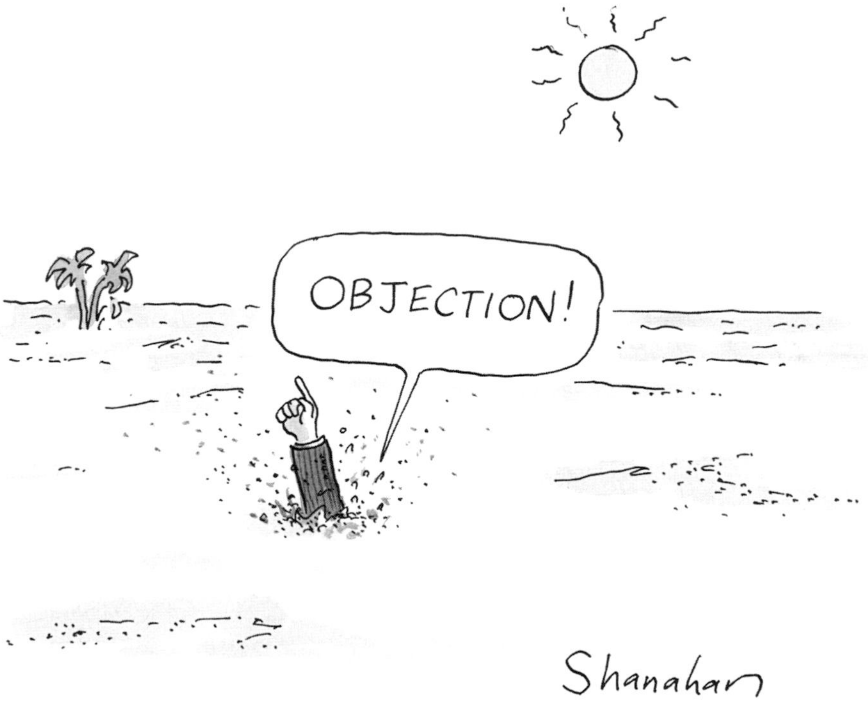
OBJECTION!
Shanahan

LAWYER OF ARABIA

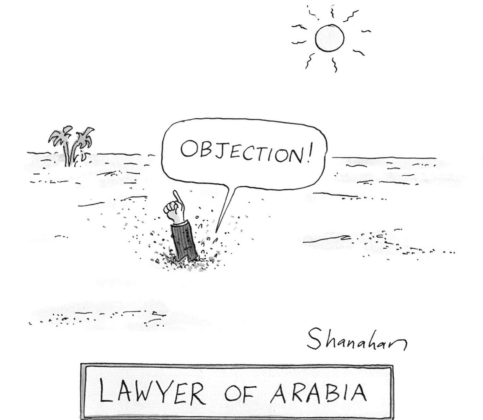

THE LAW OF THE CONCRETE JUNGLE

*If you change your mind, Replansky, we'll be down at the senior partners' swimmin' hole."*

"*Impartiality becomes you.*"

Shanahan

"Can you recommend something for the attorney who got me everything?"

Shanahan

"And now I'd like to finalize our little deal by having my attorneys scent mark your office."

"Tell us the one about swift justice, Grandpa."

*"There, there Mrs. Macklin—don't cry on billable time."*

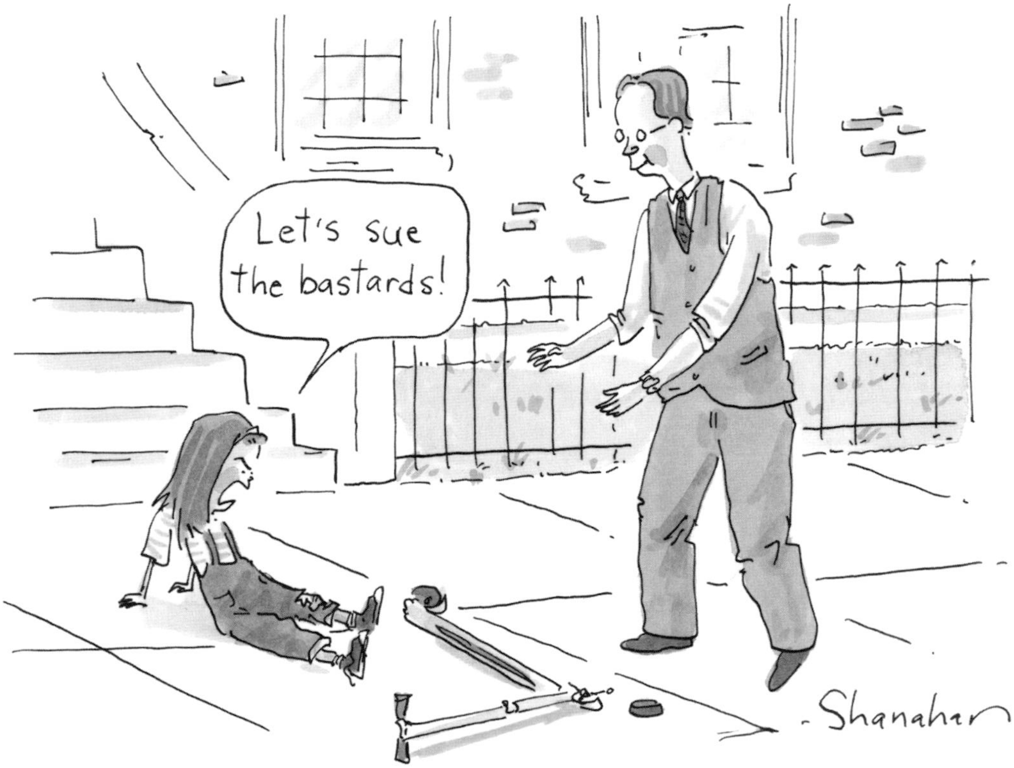
Let's sue the bastards!
Shanahan

DADDY'S LITIGIOUS GIRL

"I'll leave the door open and the hallway light on, but you're much too old to need an attorney in your room."

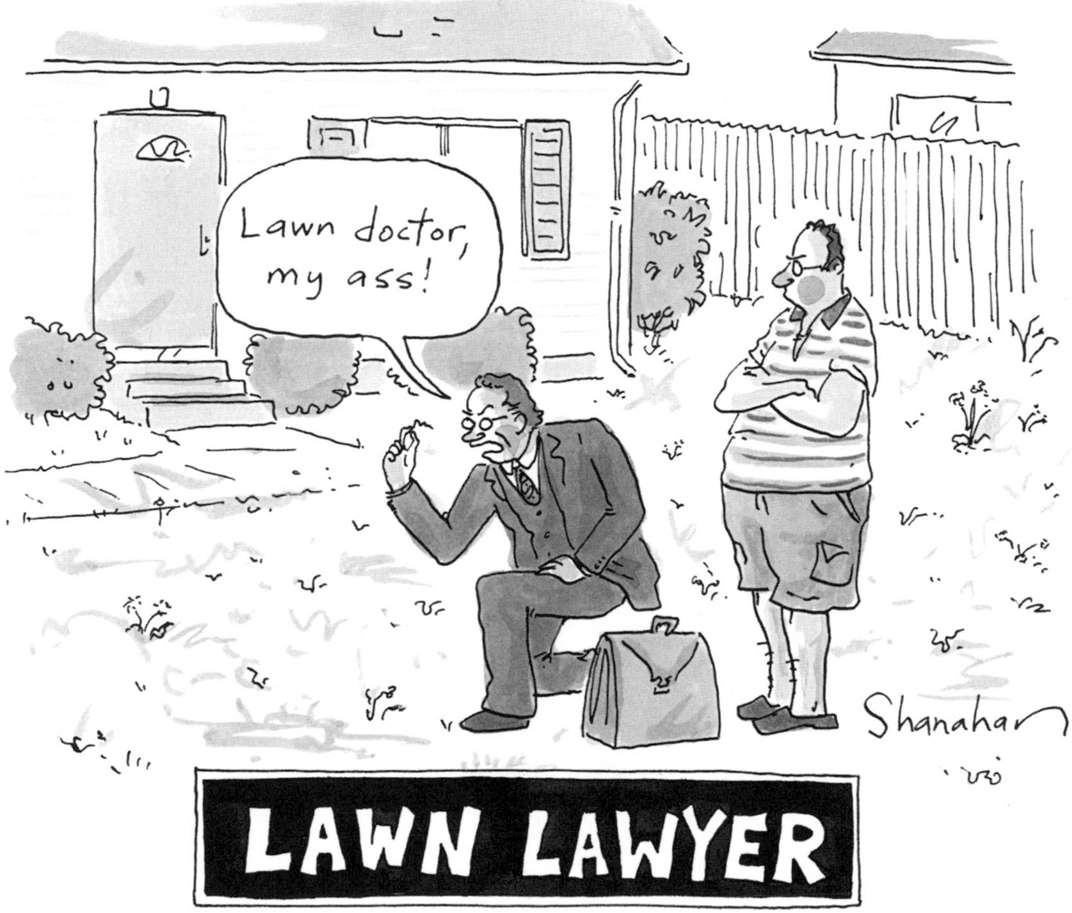
Lawn doctor, my ass!
Shanahan

LAWN LAWYER

"*Your Honor, the state has every reason to consider the defendant an extremely high flight risk.*"

Shanahan

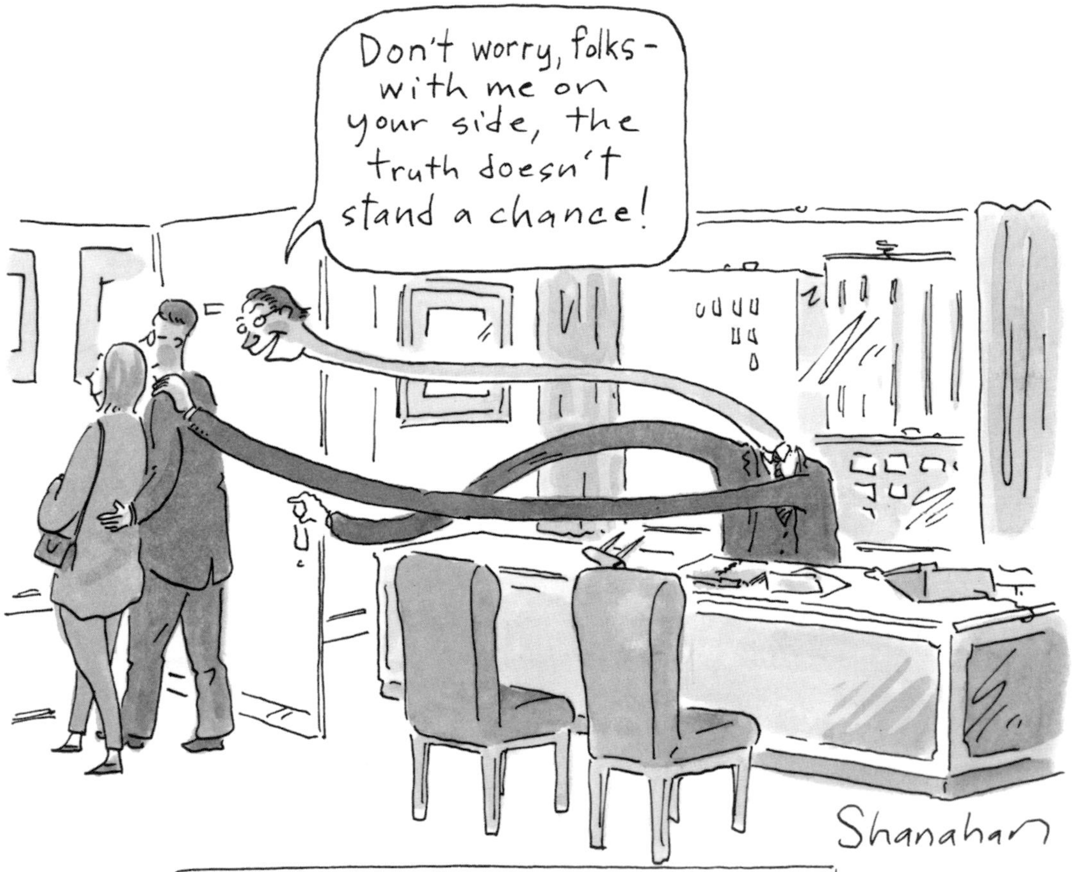
Don't worry, folks - with me on your side, the truth doesn't stand a chance!
Shanahan

SUPERPOWER OF ATTORNEY

*"Geese fly in a V, son—attorneys fly in a wedge."*

Shanahan

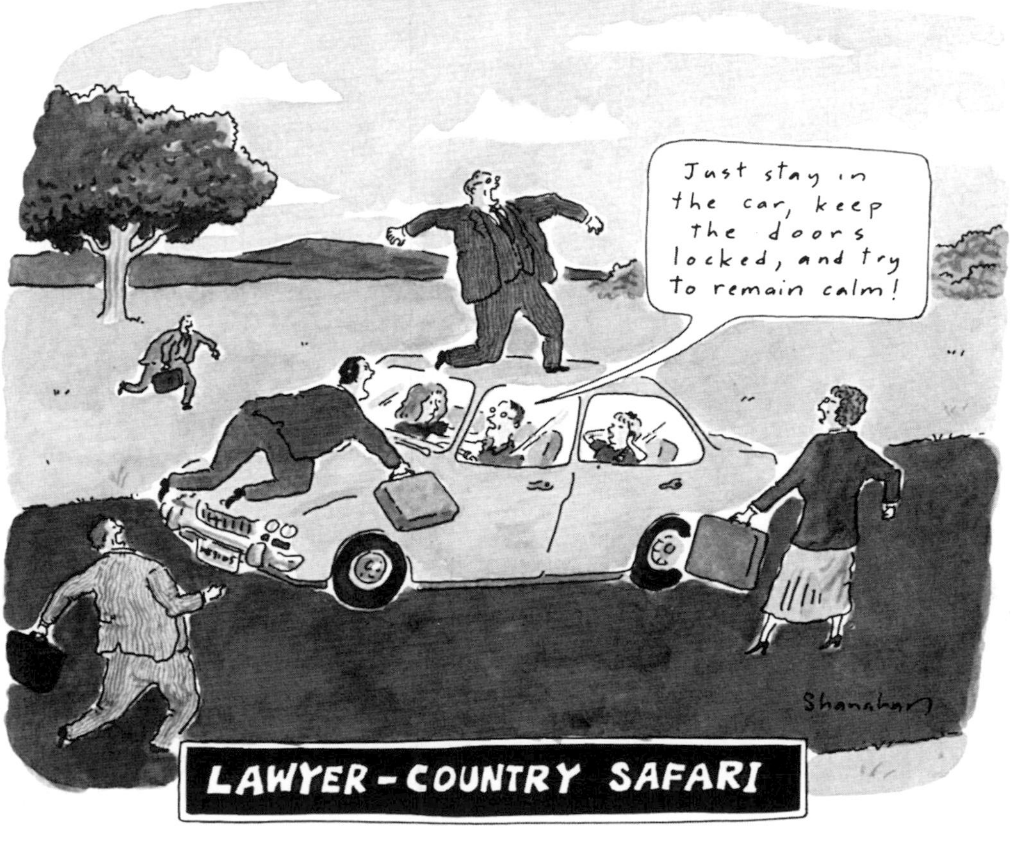
Just stay in the car, keep the doors locked, and try to remain calm!
Shanahan
LAWYER-COUNTRY SAFARI

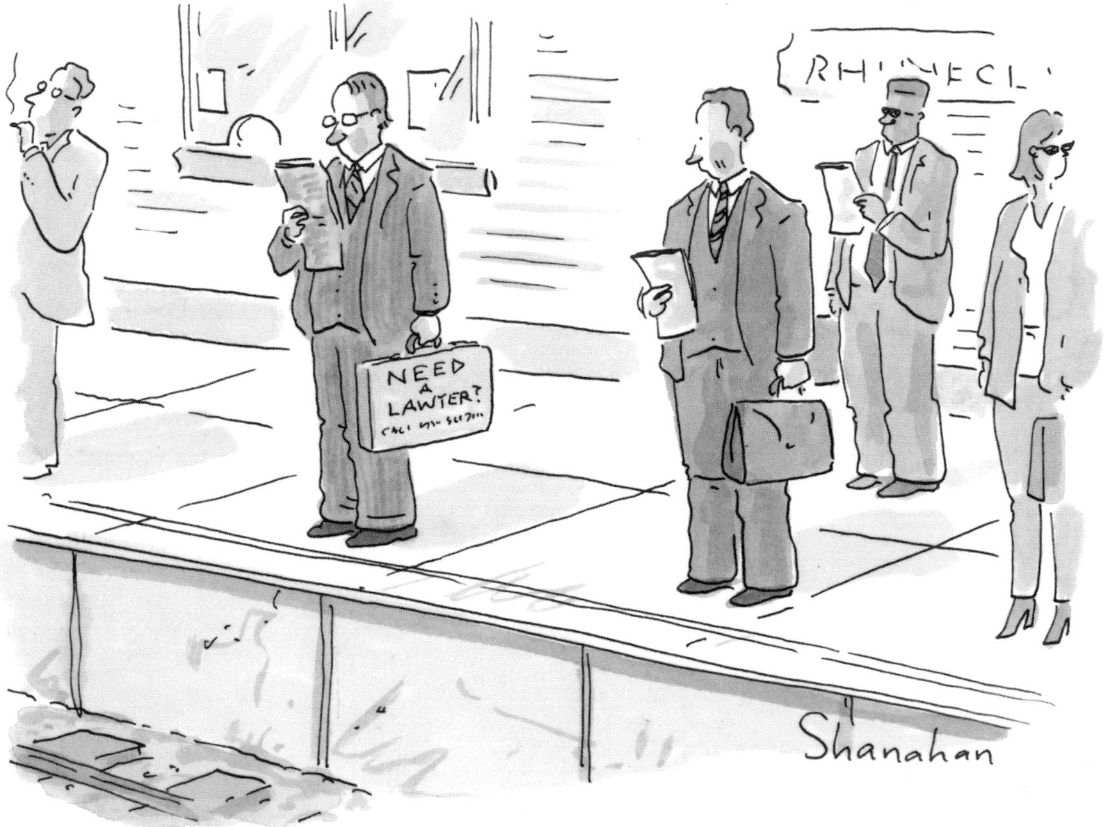
NEED A LAWYER?
Shanahan